21 CHART H|

GW00374030

WISE PUBLICATIONS
PART OF THE MUSIC SALES GROUP
LONDON / NEW YORK / PARIS / SYDNEY / COPENHAGEN / BERLIN / MADRID / HONG KONG / TOKYO

Published by

WISE PUBLICATIONS
14-15 Berners Street, London W1T 3LJ, UK.

Exclusive Distributors:

MUSIC SALES LIMITED
Distribution Centre, Newmarket Road,
Bury St Edmunds, Suffolk IP33 3YB, UK.

MUSIC SALES PTY LIMITED
20 Resolution Drive,
Caringbah, NSW 2229, Australia.

Order No. AM1001770
ISBN 978-1-84938-726-2
This book © Copyright 2010 Wise Publications,
a division of Music Sales Limited.

Edited by Jenni Wheeler.

Printed in the EU.

www.musicsales.com

YOUR GUARANTEE OF QUALITY

As publishers, we strive to produce every book
to the highest commercial standards.

The music has been freshly engraved and the book has
been carefully designed to minimise awkward page turns
and to make playing from it a real pleasure.

Particular care has been given to specifying acid-free,
neutral-sized paper made from pulps which have not been
elemental chlorine bleached. This pulp is from farmed
sustainable forests and was produced with special regard
for the environment.

Throughout, the printing and binding have been planned
to ensure a sturdy, attractive publication which should
give years of enjoyment.

If your copy fails to meet our high standards,
please inform us and we will gladly replace it.

Airplanes

Words & Music by Bobby Ray Simmons Jr., Tim Sommers,
Jeremy Dussolliet, Alexander Grant & Justin Franks

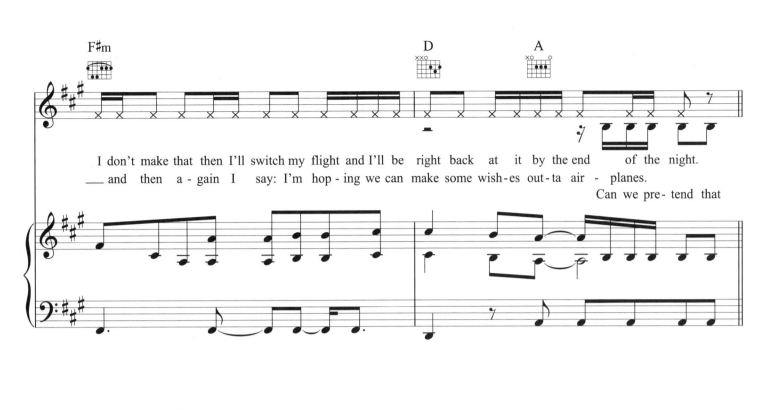

I don't make that then I'll switch my flight and I'll be right back at it by the end of the night.
___ and then a-gain I say: I'm hop-ing we can make some wish-es out-ta air - planes.
Can we pre- tend that

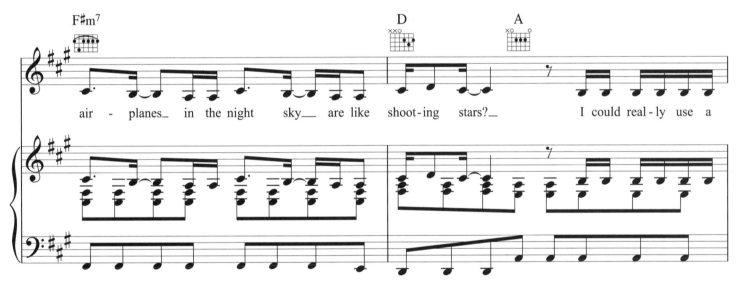

air - planes___ in the night sky___ are like shoot-ing stars?___ I could real-ly use a

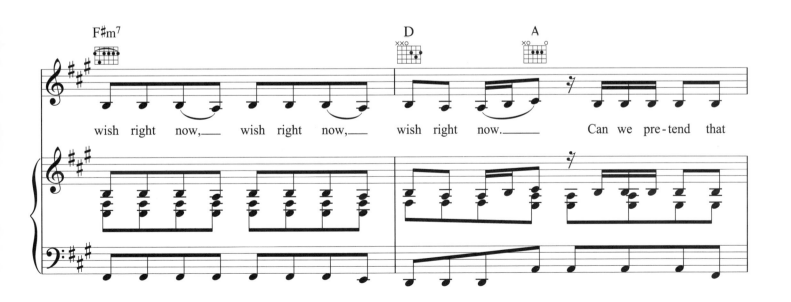

wish right now,___ wish right now,___ wish right now.___ Can we pre-tend that

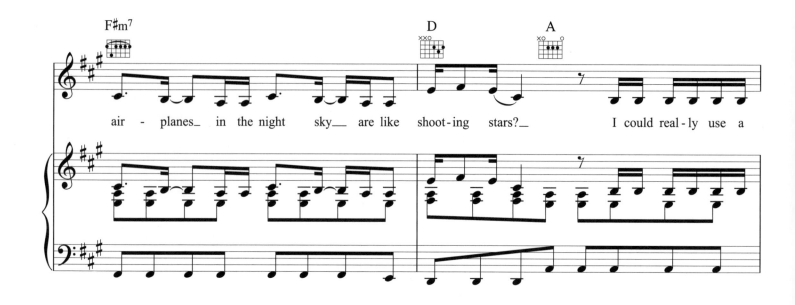

air - planes__ in the night sky__ are like shoot-ing stars?__ I could real-ly use a

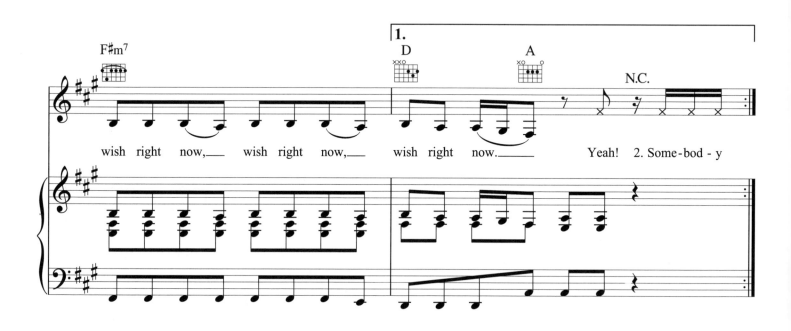

wish right now,__ wish right now,__ wish right now.__ Yeah! 2. Some-bod - y

wish right now.__ I could real-ly use a wish right now. *vocal ad lib.* I, I,

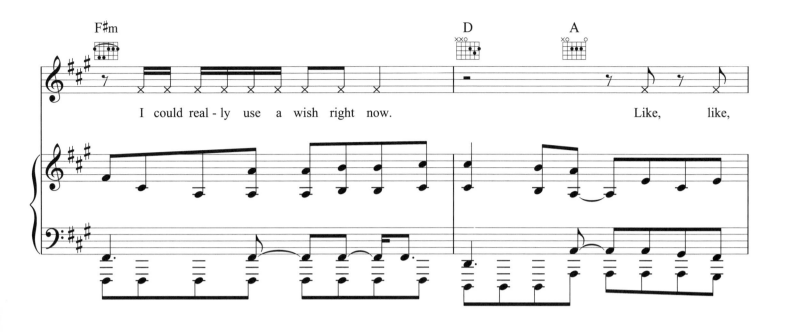

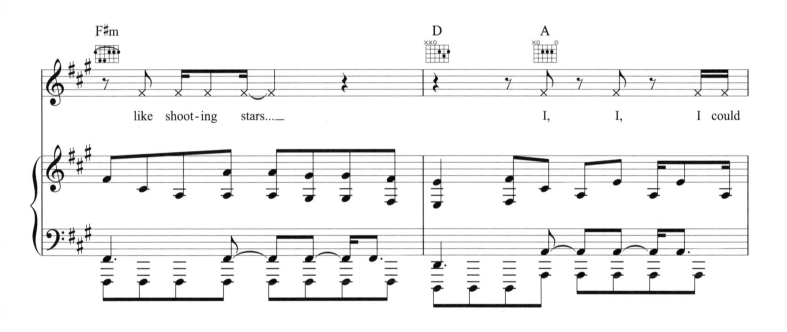

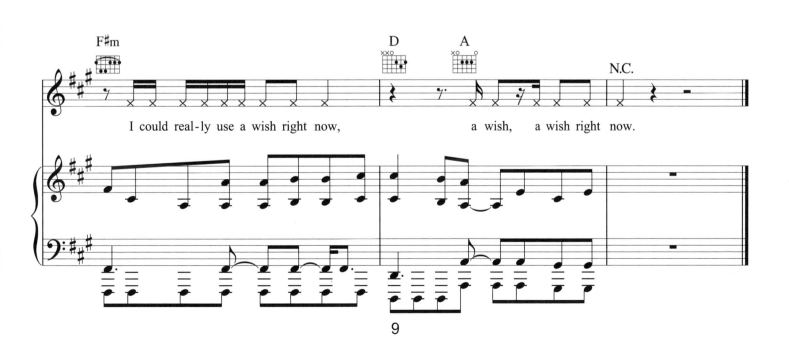

All Time Low

Words & Music by Steve Mac, Wayne Hector & Ed Drewett

Original key: B major

♩ = 132

1. Pray-ing won't do it. Hat-ing won't do it. Drink-ing won't do it. Fight-ing won't knock you out__

Beautiful Monster

Words & Music by Shaffer Smith, Tor Erik Hermansen,
Mikkel S. Eriksen & Sandy Wilhelm

1. All__ my life ... and the here - af-

-ter ... I've nev - er

seen, ... seen one like__ you.__

Fm

But I don't mind,___ in fact I___ like

it. Though I'm ter - ri - fied,___

E♭add4

I'm turned on___ but scared of___ you.___

19

said I need___ her.___ Beau-ti-ful mon-

-ster,___ but I don't___ mind.___

Oh.___ No I don't___ mind.

1.

I don't mind, I___don't, I don't___ mind. I don't mind,___ I___don't,
(No I don't___ mind.)

and she's play - ing__ with__ my mind.__

And

I don't_ mind,__ I____don't, I don't_ mind.__ No

2° with vocal ad lib.

I don't_ mind,__ I____don't, I don't_ mind.__ No

23

I don't mind,___ I___ don't, I don't mind.___ No

I don't mind,___ I___ don't, I don't mind.___ Oh.

I don't mind,___ I___ don't. Beau - ti - ful___ mon - ster.
She's a mon -

California Gurls

Words & Music by Katy Perry, Lukasz Gottwald, Max Martin,
Bonnie McKee, Benny Blanco & Calvin Broadus

Spoken: Greetings loved ones.   Let's take a journey.

1. I   know a place___   where the grass is real-ly   green - er.

Warm,   wet and wild,___   there must be some-thin' in the   wa - ter.

28

Cal - i - for - nia girls,___ we're un - de - ni - a - ble.

Fine, fresh, fierce, we got___ it on lock. West Coast rep - re - sent,___

To Coda ⊕

___ now put your hands up. Oh,___ oh.___

N.C.

Toned, tanned fit and read - y. Turn it up 'cause it's get - tin' heav - y. Wild, wild West Coast.___

These are the girls I love the most. I mean the ones, I mean like, she's the one.

Kiss her, touch her, squeeze her buns. The girl's a freak, she drive a Jeep and live on the beach.

I'm O. K. I won't play. I love the Bay, just like I love L. A., Ven-ice Beach and Palm Springs.

Sum-mer-time is ev-'ry-thing. Home-boys hang-in' out. All that ass hang-in' out. Bi-

30

31

The Cave

Words & Music by Marcus Mumford

1. It's emp-ty in the val - ley of your
(Verses 2-4 see block lyrics.)

heart, the sun it ris-es slow - ly as you walk a-way from all the fears and all the

all you want, I will not hear what you have to say. 'Cause I need

free - dom now and I need to know how to

live my life as it's meant to be.

(Ah, ah,
(Backing vocals)

Verse 2
The harvest left no food for you to eat,
You cannibal, you meat-eater, you see.
But I have seen the same,
I know the shame in your defeat.

Verse 3
'Cause I have other things to fill my time,
You take what is yours and I'll take mine.
Now let me at the truth,
Which will refresh my broken mind.

Verse 4
So tie me to a post and block my ears,
I can see widows and orphans through my tears.
And know my call despite my faults
And despite my growing fears.

Choices

Words & Music by Irwin Sparkes, Martin Skarendahl,
Alfonso Sharland, Sam Swallows & Toby Smith

more than I____ can bear. You de‑mand____ I make my mind____ up by de‑

‑cid‑ing not____ to care.____ Stop giv‑ing me choic ‑ es.____

Stop giv‑ing me choic ‑ es. 2. I'm the vic ‑ tim

of this day and age. I've for‑got ‑ ten how to feel. I've for‑got‑

Crossfire

Words & Music by Brandon Flowers

Find Your Love

Words & Music by Aubrey Graham, Kanye West, Jeff Bhasker,
Ernest Wilson & Patrick Reynolds

57

Gettin' Over You

Words & Music by David Guetta, Chris Willis, Jean-Claude Sindres,
Sandy Wilhelm & Frédéric Riesterer

62

if you've ev - er felt___ love,___ then you know, yeah, you know what I'm

talk - in' a - bout. There's no get - tin' o - ver._____

Ah._____ Ah._____ Ah._

Just Be Good To Green

Words & Music by Stephen Manderson, Andrew Hughes,
Jimmy Jam & Terry Lewis

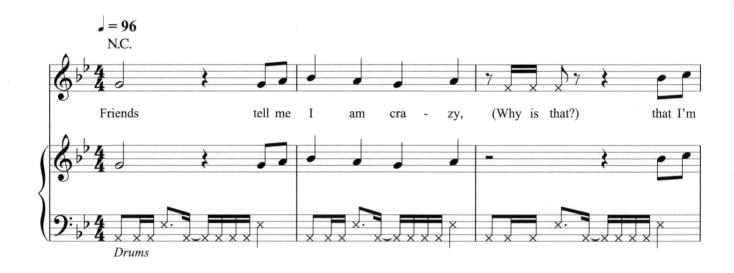

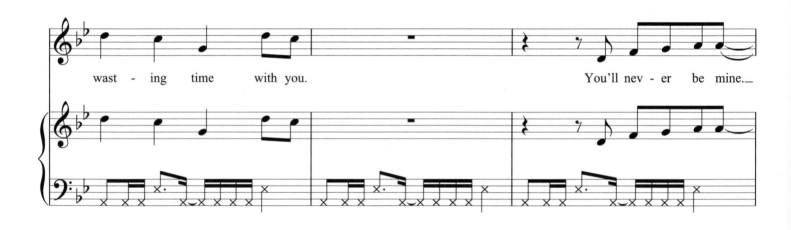

N.C.

1. Huh. Just be___ good to Green. All I need is a wom-an to be___ good to me. I'm an
(Verse 2 see block lyrics)

eas - y man. I'm eas - i - ly pleased. And you pro-vide me with ev-'ry-thing that I need. Look,

you know I make ends, I grind.___ So hold on to yours,___ we're spend-ing mine.___

Though you try I nev-er let you buy.___ But if I was broke would you still be spend - ing time?___ (Yes.)

Verse 2:

Look babes, you know who I am
But as crooked as I am
I'll be as good as I can.
I try an' try though its evident my
Angel face is disguised for the devil inside.
You're good to me, I ain't good to girls needs; me?
I'm a bad boy, something every good girl needs, heh.
Honesty could avoid all your tantrums
But I'm a naughty boy and I always have been.
What?
An' that ain't changing any time soon.

I can't have you with me whenever I move
Whatever I do, I come back to you.
See, the good attracts me and the crook attracts you
Whatever.
What?
We've all got our ways
Remember us talking?
Of course it was game
But it's all gone and changed.
Now she's got me cutting off links
Like I'm trying to shorten my chain.

Love The Way You Lie

Words & Music by Marshall Mathers, Alexander Grant & H. Hafferman

because I like the way it hurts. Just gon-na

stand there and hear me cry. But that's al - right

because I love the way you lie. I love the way you

lie. I love the way you

lie.

Verse 2:

You ever love somebody so much you can barely breathe?
When you with 'em you meet and neither one of you even know what hit 'em.
Got that warm fuzzy feeling
Yeah, them those chills used to get 'em
Now you're getting fuckin' sick of lookin' at him.
You swore you'd never hit 'em, never do nothin' to hurt him
Now you're in each other's face spewin' venom in your words when you spit 'em.
You push pull each other's hair,
Scratch claw hit him throw him down pin him,
So lost in the moments when you're in 'em.
It's the rage that took over, it controls you both
So they say you're the best to go your separate ways.
Guess if they don't know you 'cause today that was yesterday,
Yesterday is over, it's a different day.
Sound like broken records playing over but you promised her
Next time you show restraint, you don't get another chance.
Life is no Nintendo game but you lied again
Now you get to watch her leave out the window,
I guess that's why they call it window pane.

Verse 3:

Now I know we said things, hit things that we didn't mean
And we fall back into the same patterns same routine.
But your temper's just as bad as mine is,
You're the same as me.
But when it comes to love you're just as blinded.
Baby, please come back it wasn't you, baby it was me,
Maybe our relationship isn't as crazy as it seems.
Maybe that's what happens when a tornado meets a volcano,
All I know is I love you too much to walk away though.
Come inside, pick up your bags off the sidewalk,
Don't you hear sincerity in my voice when I talk?
I told you this is my fault,
Look me in the eyeball
Next time I'm pissed, I'll aim my fist at the drywall.
Next time. There won't be no next time,
I apologize even though I know its lies.
I'm tired of the games I just want her back.
I know I'm a liar,
If she ever tries to fucking leave again
I'm-a tie her to the bed and set this house on fire.

OMG

Words & Music by Will Adams

84

Pack Up

Words & Music by Eliza Caird, Tim Woodcock, Matthew Prime,
Felix Powell & George Asaf

Prayin'

Words & Music by Benjamin Ballance-Drew, Eric Appapoulay,
Richard Cassell & Tom Goss

Solo

Words & Music by Keidran Jones, Jonathan Rotem, August Rigo,
Jason Desrouleaux, James Harris III, Terry Lewis & Janet Jackson

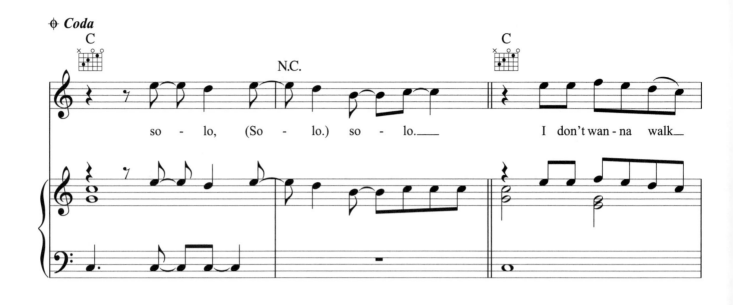

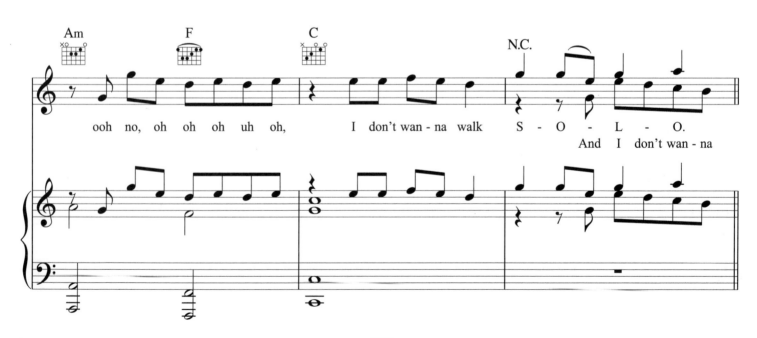

Ridin' Solo

Words & Music by Jason Desrouleaux & Jonathan Rotem

106

Turn It Up

Words & Music by Pixie Lott, Ruth Anne Cunningham,
Jonas Jeberg & Mich Hansen

Te Amo

Words & Music by Mikkel S. Eriksen, Tor Erik Hermansen,
James Fauntleroy II & Robyn Fenty

1. "Te a - mo, te a - mo." She says to me
2. "Te a - mo, te a - mo." She's scared to breathe.
(you?)

Telephone

Words & Music by Stefani Germanotta, Rodney Jerkins, LaShawn Daniels,
Lazonate Franklin & Beyoncé Knowles

out in the club, and I'm sip-ping that bub, and you're not gon-na reach my te - le - phone.

My te - le - phone, my te - le - phone; I'm out in the club, and I'm sip-ping that bub, and you're

not gon-na reach my te - le - phone.

Spoken:
We're sorry, (We're sorry.) the number you have

reached is not in service at this time. Please check the number, or try your call again.

We No Speak Americano

Words by Nicola Salerno
Music by Renato Carosone
Arranged by Johnson Peterson, Sylvester Martinez & Duncan MacLennan

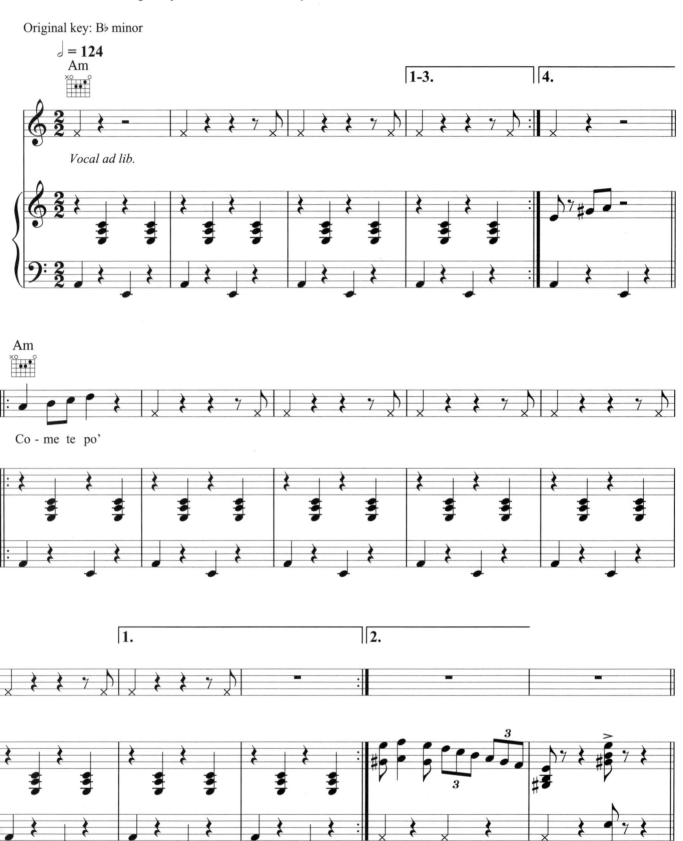

-ca - no.

Fa' fa' ll'a-me-ri - ca-no.

Fa' fa' ll'a-me-ri - ca - no.

roll. Whis-ky so-da e rock and roll.

Weightless

Words & Music by Alex Gaskarth, Matthew Squire, Jack Barakat,
Rian Dawson & Zack Merrick

139

Bringing you the words and the music

All the latest music in print... rock & pop plus jazz, blues, country, classical and the best in West End show scores.

- Books to match your favourite CDs.

- Book-and-CD titles with high quality backing tracks for you to play along to. Now you can play guitar or piano with your favourite artist... or simply sing along!

- Audition songbooks with CD backing tracks for both male and female singers for all those with stars in their eyes.

- Can't read music? No problem, you can still play all the hits with our wide range of chord songbooks.

- Check out our range of instrumental tutorial titles, taking you from novice to expert in no time at all!

- Musical show scores include *The Phantom Of The Opera*, *Les Misérables*, *Mamma Mia* and many more hit productions.

- DVD master classes featuring the techniques of top artists.